EXTREME EARTH

LOWEST PLACES
ON THE PLANET

by Karen Soll

raintree
a Capstone company — publishers for children

Raintree is an imprint of Capstone Global Library Limited, a company incorporated in England and Wales having its registered office at 264 Banbury Road, Oxford, OX2 7DY – Registered company number: 6695582

www.raintree.co.uk
myorders@raintree.co.uk

Editorial Credits
Karen Soll, editor; Juliette Peters, designer;
Tracy Cummins, media specialist; Tori Abraham, production specialist

ISBN 978 1 4747 1266 8
20 19 18 17 16 15
10 9 8 7 6 5 4 3 2 1

British Library Cataloguing in Publication Data
A full catalogue record for this book is available from the British Library.

Photo Credits
Alamy: Dmytro Pylypenko, 19; Corbis: Luo Sha/Xinhua Press, 21; Marcelo Kovacic: 13; Shutterstock: Avik, 3, 11, 22-23, Endless Traveller, 15, Felix Lipov, Cover Bottom Left, Ivsanmas, Map, Nickolay Vinokurov, Cover Top, 17, Ovidiu Hrubaru, 5, S. Bonaime, Cover Bottom Right, Vadim Petrakov, Design Element, 1; Thinkstock: Anatoly Ustinenko, 9, Quinn Rooney, 7

Every effort has been made to contact copyright holders of material reproduced in this book. Any omissions will be rectified in subsequent printings if notice is given to the publisher.

All the internet addresses (URLs) given in this book were valid at the time of going to press. However, due to the dynamic nature of the internet, some addresses may have changed, or sites may have changed or ceased to exist since publication. While the author and publisher regret any inconvenience this may cause readers, no responsibility for any such changes can be accepted by either the author or the publisher.

Note to Parents and Teachers

The Extreme Earth set supports topics related to earth science. This book describes and illustrates climate and geography. The images support early readers in understanding the text. The repetition of words and phrases helps early readers learn new words. This book also introduces early readers to subject-specific vocabulary, which is defined in the Glossary section. Early readers may need assistance to read some words and to use the Table of contents, Glossary, Read more, Websites, Critical thinking questions, and Index sections of the book.

Printed and bound in China.

CONTENTS

LOW PLACES

Tall hills and high places
are all around. The ground
dips low in other places.
Let's find out about these
low places.

One lake in Australia
is very low. Rain can fill it.
Then it is the biggest lake
in Australia.

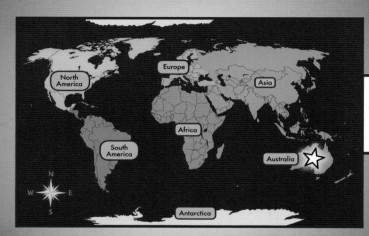

Lake Eyre is 16 metres (52 feet)
below sea level.

There is a body of water
between Europe and Asia.
This is Europe's lowest point.
It is also the largest lake
in the world.

The Caspian Sea is 28 metres
(92 feet) below sea level.

LOWER PLACES

Death Valley is in California.

It is the lowest place

in North America.

It is hot and dry too.

Death Valley is 86 metres
(282 feet) below sea level.

South America has

a lake as its lowest point.

Many rivers drain into it.

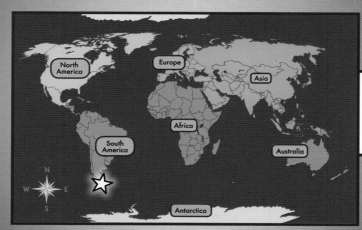

Laguna del Carbón is 105 metres (344 feet) below sea level.

The lowest place in Africa is a lake too! It gets very hot here. The heat turns the water into a gas.

Lake Assal is 155 metres (509 feet) below sea level.

LOWEST PLACES

The lowest point in Asia
is by the Dead Sea.

It is the shore.

The shoreline of the Dead Sea
is 415 metres (1,360 feet) below
sea level.

One trench in Antarctica is the lowest point in the world that water does not cover. It is cold and icy.

The Bentley Subglacial Trench in Antarctica is 2,540 metres (8,333 feet) below sea level.

The Pacific Ocean

has the lowest point.

Only special boats go there.

Would you like to see any

of these low places?

The Mariana Trench is 11,033 metres (36,198 feet) below sea level.

GLOSSARY

Africa—a continent between the Atlantic and Indian Oceans and south of Europe

Asia—a large continent that contains many countries, including China and India

Australia—a continent in the South Pacific Ocean

Dead Sea—a large salt lake between Israel and Jordan

drain—to flow into something

Europe—a continent west of Asia

North America—a continent in the Western Hemisphere that includes the United States, Canada, Mexico and Central America

sea level—the average level of the surface of the ocean, used as a starting point from which to measure the height or depth of any place

shore—the place where water meets land

South America—a continent between the Atlantic and Pacific Oceans

READ MORE

Earth's Lowest Places (Earth's Most Extreme Places), Bailey O'Connell (Gareth Stevens Publishing, 2015)

Oceans and Seas (Discover Science), Nicola Davies (Kingfisher, 2011)

Seymour Simon's Extreme Earth Records, Seymour Simon (Chronicle Books, 2012)

WEBSITES

http://www.nps.gov/deva/learn/nature/lowest-places-on-earth.htm
Discover and compare some of the lowest places on earth.

http://education.nationalgeographic.com/education/encyclopedia/sea-level/?ar_a=1
Learn about sea level and things that can make it change.

http://kids.britannica.com/comptons/article-9273934/Dead-Sea
Find out all about the Dead Sea.

CRITICAL THINKING QUESTIONS

1. Look at the picture on page 19, and read the text. Why might Antarctica have a low point that water does not cover?

2. The author says that many rivers drain into a lake in South America. What does it mean for a river to drain into a lake?

3. Heat can turn the water in Africa's lake to a gas. Write about what happens to the water.

INDEX